CARVING PUMPKINS

By Dana Meachen Rau • Illustrated by Kathleen Pete

CHERRY LAKE PUBLISHING • ANN ARBOR, M

CHERRY
LAKE
Publishing

Published in the United States of America by Cherry Lake Publishing
Ann Arbor, Michigan
www.cherrylakepublishing.com

Content Adviser: Dr. Julia Hovanec, Department of Arts Education and
Crafts, Kutztown University of Pennsylvania, Kutztown, Pennsylvania

Photo Credits: Page 4, ©Christian Jung/Dreamstime.com; page 5,
©Lastdays1/Dreamstime.com; page 10, ©James Steidl/Dreamstime
.com; page 12, ©Juan Carlos Tinjaca/Dreamstime.com; page 16,
©Bronwyn8/Dreamstime.com; page 18, ©Maunger/Dreamstime.com;
page 20, ©Begepotam/Dreamstime.com; pages 27 and 28, ©Dana
Meachen Rau, page 32, Tania McNaboe

Library of Congress Cataloging-in-Publication Data
Rau, Dana Meachen, 1971–
  Carving pumpkins / by Dana Meachen Rau.
p. cm.
Includes bibliographical references and index.
ISBN 978-1-61080-470-7 (lib. bdg.)—
ISBN 978-1-61080-557-5 (e-book) — ISBN 978-1-61080-644-2 (pbk.)
1. Jack-o-lanterns—Juvenile literature. 2. Halloween decorations—
Juvenile literature. I. Title.
  TT900.H32R36 2012
  745.594'1646—dc23   2012001734

Cherry Lake Publishing would like to acknowledge the work
of The Partnership for 21st Century Skills. Please visit
www.21stcenturyskills.org for more information.

Printed in the United States of America
Corporate Graphics Inc.
July 2012
CLFA11

A NOTE TO ADULTS:
Please review the instructions for these craft projects before your children make them. Be sure to help them with any crafts you do not think they can safely conduct on their own.

A NOTE TO KIDS:
Be sure to ask an adult for help with these craft activities when you need it. Always put your safety first!

HOW-TO
LIBRARY

TABLE OF CONTENTS

Perfect Pumpkins

In autumn, pumpkins pop up everywhere! Just like sculptors use clay, you can carve pumpkins into interesting shapes, scenes, and characters. You just need some tools and your imagination.

Pumpkins come in many colors and shapes. You'll find orange, red, green, and white pumpkins. They can be tall, short, flat, or bumpy.

Pumpkins come in many colors and shapes.

- Jack-o'-lantern pumpkins are a deep orange color and are the best ones for carving. Some varieties include Connecticut Field and Howden. They have tall walls, thin flesh, and sturdy **stems**.
- Lumina pumpkins are white on the outside. They have orange flesh on the inside.
- Jack Be Littles are tiny and make great decorations.

You can find jack-o'-lantern pumpkins in many different places in the fall.

There are a lot of other varieties, too, such as short, fat Fairytales or green-gray Jarrahdales. Some of these are better for baking and have a thick **skin** that's harder to carve. This fall, shop for pumpkins at grocery stores, roadside stands, farms, and fairs. Keep your eye out for the perfect one to express your creative ideas.

DID YOU KNOW?
Pumpkins are fruits. Fruits are the parts of plants that hold the seeds.

Tricky Jack

Carved pumpkins are called jack-o'-lanterns.

People place jack-o'-lanterns in windows. They also place them on porches to greet visitors. This is a tradition around the fall holidays.

The jack-o'-lantern tradition started with an old Irish legend about a man named Jack. Jack was a tricky man. When he died, heaven would not let him in. The devil didn't want him either. He was left to wander in darkness. All he had was a burning piece of coal for light. He placed it in a lantern carved from a turnip. He became known as "Jack of the lantern" or "Jack-o'-lantern."

To keep Jack's wandering spirit away, people carved scary faces in turnips, potatoes, and even beets. They placed the carvings in their windows and on their doorsteps.

In the 1800s, many Irish immigrants came to America. They brought their traditions with them. They found that the pumpkin, a fruit **native** to America, was easy to carve. It made the perfect jack-o'-lantern.

When Irish immigrants came to America, they carved pumpkins to keep the wandering spirit of Jack away.

Basic Tools

Stores sell pumpkin-carving kits. Your kitchen, toolbox, or toy box may also hold tools you can use to make your pumpkin come alive. Below are some of the tools you can use.

Planning Tools
Paper

Pencil

Pushpin or nail

Grease pencil

Scooping Tools
Long-handled
  spoon

Ice cream scoop

Bowl

Carving Tools
Sharp knife

Thin saw

Apple corer

Cookie cutters

Electric drill

Melon baller

Linoleum cutters

Lights
Votive candles and
  holders

Battery-powered
  lights

Decorations
Low-temperature
  glue gun

Paints or markers

Natural items
  such as gourds,
  branches, nuts,
  or leaves

Toys and candy

Clothing or other
  accessories

SAFETY FIRST

Always get an adult's permission and supervision when using a knife, saw, or other carving tools. Cut away from your body, and be sure your other hand is not in the way. Sharp tools are often safer than dull ones. For example, a dull knife can skim across the surface of the pumpkin, cutting you by mistake. A sharp knife will more likely go where you want it to go—into the fruit and not into you!

Picking Your Pumpkin

You can find a pumpkin that is just right for you!

No two pumpkins are exactly the same. You may have a design in mind. If so, you may already know what shape that you want to buy. Or the pumpkin you find may inspire you. Either way, you'll know the perfect one when you see it!

Look for a pumpkin that is the same color and shape all the way around. Test to see if it stands up straight. You might want one with skin that does not have too many knobs or bumps. Or maybe you want the bumpiest one you can get!

Don't buy a pumpkin with soft spots or bruises. These areas will rot sooner than the rest and won't stand up well to carving.

Never carry your pumpkin by its stem. Support it from the bottom instead. The stem may feel strong, but it can break off and send your pumpkin crashing to the ground.

At home, you should store your pumpkin in a cool place like a porch or patio until you're ready to carve it. A fresh pumpkin will last a month or more before it starts to rot. But a carved one only lasts about 5 to 10 days. Carve it 1 or 2 days before you plan to display it.

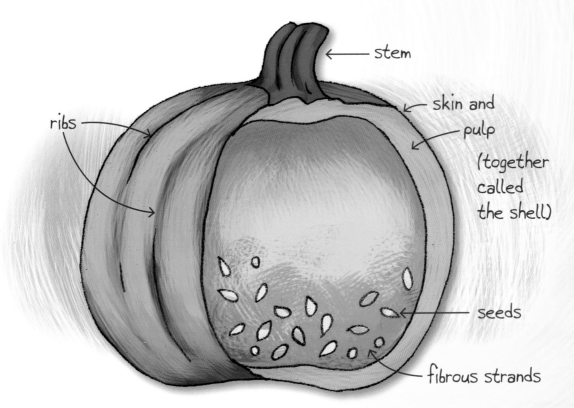

stem

skin and pulp

(together called the shell)

ribs

seeds

fibrous strands

Making a Plan

You should sketch some ideas before you carve.

Artists often make sketches before they start a final piece of art. You should make a plan before you start carving your pumpkin, too. A sketch is a good place to work out your ideas and solve any problems before you make the first cut.

Brainstorm a bunch of ideas. Then draw one out in actual size with paper and a pencil. The simpler the image, the easier it will be to carve. You can buy pre-drawn images, but it is usually more fun to make your own.

You can draw your image right onto the pumpkin's skin with a grease pencil. Or you can **transfer** the image onto your pumpkin. Here's how:

Step One: Cut out your picture and tape it to the front of your pumpkin. Try to tape it as flat as you can.

Step Two: With a pin or nail, poke through the paper into the pumpkin's skin. Follow along the lines of your image, poking dots every quarter to half an inch (0.5–1.25 centimeters). Be sure you don't miss any lines.

Step Three: Remove the paper. Your image is now drawn in little dots. Now you'll know exactly where to cut.

LISTEN TO THE PUMPKIN
If you're having trouble thinking of ideas, let the pumpkin "speak" to you. What does it want to be? If it's cute and round, maybe it wants to have a happy face. A white one may be good for a ghost. A green one might make a good frog. Is your pumpkin huge? It may have lots of room for a more detailed design.

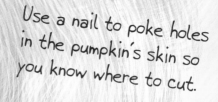

Use a nail to poke holes in the pumpkin's skin so you know where to cut.

Pumpkin Personalities

Do you want your pumpkin to welcome guests with a friendly smile? Or do you want it to scare them away? How you choose to arrange its eyes, nose, and mouth will give the pumpkin its personality.

Eyes, eyebrows, and noses can be circles and triangles, or a mix of both. Eyes or eyebrows that slant down on the inside make your pumpkin look angry or scary. Eyes that slant down on the outside can make it look sad or worried. Above are some examples.

Mouths can be big, small, turned up, turned down, or include teeth and fangs. The size of the mouth expresses personality, too. A small mouth with fangs is scary. A huge mouth with fangs is even scarier!

Pumpkins can be pets. Think about your animal's features. Here are some examples:

MIX AND MATCH
Combine different eyes and mouths to give your pumpkin a unique personality!

Scooping the Goop

Spread newspaper over your workspace. You might also cover your work area with cardboard or wood to protect it from spills or scratches. If you can work outside, that's even better. If your pumpkin is dirty from sitting in soil at the pumpkin patch, scrub it gently with your hand and some water, and then dry it.

Cleaning out a pumpkin can be messy.

Cutting shapes out of the pumpkin isn't easy. The **shell**, which includes the orange skin and the inside **pulp**, is thick. A sharp knife or thin saw works best. Don't forget to get an adult's permission and supervision when using these tools.

Step One: Cut a Lid

Cut a circle around the top of your pumpkin with the stem in the center. Angle the knife as you cut so your lid won't fall in. Make the hole big enough for you to reach in easily. If you'd rather keep the top of your pumpkin smooth, cut a rectangle in the back as a trapdoor instead.

Step Two: Get Out the Goop

The inside of the pumpkin is filled with slimy strands and seeds. Use a plastic or metal long-handled cooking spoon. Scrape the spoon along the inside of the shell and scoop out the goop. You can also use an ice cream scoop. As you work, place all the goop in a bowl. Later you can dump this in the woods or toast the seeds for a crunchy, healthy snack.

Step Three: Smooth It Out

You want the pumpkin to look like a smooth bowl inside. Scrape the inside walls to about 1-inch (2.5 cm) thick. You can use an eating spoon to scrape small areas. A grapefruit spoon works well, too, because it has a **serrated** tip. Pay extra attention to the bottom of the pumpkin bowl. It will have a **nub** where the blossom grew while the pumpkin was on the vine. Your light will have to sit on this spot, so give it a few extra scrapes to be sure it is flat.

Carving Tips

Be sure to carve slowly and carefully.

Now you can start carving. Ask an adult to help you with all the carving tools. It is very dangerous to use them by yourself.

Put the tip of your knife on your dotted line, push through the shell, and follow the line to make a clean cut.

MAKE MISTAKES WORK!
If you mess up while you're carving, don't worry. Think of ways to change your design as you go. Use a toothpick to reattach a piece of pumpkin if you cut it off by mistake. Your "mistake" might end up making your project even better!

When you use a saw, move it in and out along the line. After you cut out areas, use the knife or saw to smooth out curves.

An apple corer is a good tool for making small holes. Push it into the pumpkin and pull it out. You can also use an electric drill to cut round holes. Different drill bits make different-size holes.

A metal cookie cutter can help cut a specific shape. Place it on the pumpkin's shell and push it in until it goes through the other side.

You don't have to cut all parts of your design through the entire shell. You can carve in just far enough for light to shine out, but not so far that you poke through the pulp. A melon baller is a good tool to scoop round shapes out of the skin. Linoleum cutters have sharp curved ends. They are good for carving off the skin, too.

Be sure to wash and dry all of the tools when you finish.

LIGHT IT UP

Candles or battery-powered lights can make your pumpkin shine. If you use a candle, place it in a glass holder. This will help your candle stand up, give off more light, and burn longer.

Open the pumpkin's lid or trapdoor and place the light inside. Make sure it sits level on the bottom. You can also cut a hole in the bottom of the pumpkin and place the whole thing over the light. Light the candle after it is placed in the pumpkin. Keep the lid or trapdoor open so the candle's heat can vent out.

Never leave a flame or light unattended. If you are going to bed or leaving the house, be sure to blow out or turn off the light.

Adding Details

What details will help your pumpkin come to life?

You don't have to carve all the details on your pumpkin. Add clothing, accessories, or other items to create an interesting design. If you use any items that can catch fire, use a battery-powered light instead of a candle.

Natural Decorations

Look around your yard, garden, or nearby park for bits of nature. Branches make good pumpkin arms. Hay can be hair. Think of ways to use acorns, gourds, pinecones, dried corn, and flowers. You can even build an autumn snowman by stacking three pumpkins, adding natural decorations, and using an overturned clay pot as a top hat.

Candy

Candy can be a colorful and fun way to add details. Candy corn looks a lot like teeth. Lollipops look like insect antennae. Attach candy to the pumpkin using toothpicks or a low-temperature glue gun.

Clothing

Dress up your pumpkin with a baseball cap, football helmet, or knit winter hat. Give it feet by placing it on top of two old sneakers. Decorate it with a swim cap, sunglasses, and scuba flippers for a beach bum pumpkin.

Jack-o'-lanterns are often used as scarecrow heads. Stuff an old shirt and pants with hay, and sit the scarecrow in a lawn chair. Place the pumpkin where its head should be.

Craft Items

Pipe cleaners, paint, markers, and anything you use for craft projects can be used to decorate pumpkins, too.

PUMPKIN PARTY
Invite some friends over and have a carving party. Ask them to bring their ideas and supplies so everyone can share in the planning and fun.

Hanging Lantern

This hanging lantern will add light to your walkway, garden, or other outdoor space.

Materials:

Jute or macramé cord
Ruler
Scissors
Small pumpkin
Scooping and carving tools (*see pages 8–9*)
Battery-powered light

Steps:

1. Measure and cut the cord into 6 pieces, each 10 feet (3 meters) long. Fold the pieces in half. Gather them together.
2. At the folded end, tie an overhand knot so that you have a loop and 12 cords hanging down. Hook the loop onto a doorknob.
3. Untangle the cords into four groups of three. Braid one group together until the braid is about 12 inches (30 cm) long. Then tie an overhand knot at the end of the braid. Repeat with the other three sets of cords.

4. Take two cords from the end of one braid and one cord from the braid next to it. Tie these together with an overhand knot about 4 inches (10 cm) down. Repeat with the other three sets of cords.

5. Bring all the cords back together and tie in an overhand knot about 6 inches (15 cm) down.

6. Place your pumpkin in the holder and adjust the knots if needed. Braid the extra cords and knot the ends.

7. With a grease pencil, draw diamond and circle shapes in the open spaces of the pumpkin. Take it out of the holder and carve as described on pages 18–19.

8. Place your pumpkin in the holder and hang outdoors. Depending on the size and weight of the pumpkin, you can hang it on a tree branch or garden hook. Add a light at night and let it shine.

step 2 ⟶

step 3 ⟶

step 4

step 5

step 7

←step 6

23

Alien Encounter

Look what's landed in the backyard! A glowing group of aliens and their ship have stopped by to visit.

ALIEN ARMY
Carve lots of little white pumpkins and place them around your ship to look like an alien army!

Materials:

3 small, white pumpkins

1 tall, large pumpkin

Planning, scooping, and carving tools (*see pages 8–9*)

6 glow sticks

3 battery-powered lights

Strobe light

Steps:

1. Prepare all the pumpkins for carving by following the directions on pages 16–17. However, do not cut top lids. Instead, cut trapdoors in the back.

2. Sketch out your design for your aliens' features—big eyes, small nostrils, and a mouth. Transfer the designs onto your white pumpkins (*see directions on pages 12–13*). Then carve the features by following the carving tips on pages 18–19.

3. For the spaceship, place the large pumpkin on its side. Cut squares around the middle of the whole pumpkin. With a drill or large nail, make a line of holes above and below your squares. Add some triangle shapes above and below your lines of holes.

4. To light your aliens, poke two glow sticks into the top of each one to look like antennae. Place battery-powered lights inside each one through the trapdoors in the back.

5. To light the ship, place a strobe light inside.

Haunted House Display

Nothing is spookier than a haunted house. Make this multi-pumpkin display by adding lots of natural decorations.

Materials:

1 tall, large pumpkin

5 small pumpkins, all about the same size

Planning, scooping, and carving tools (*see pages 8–9*)

Hay or dried grass

Glue

Small branches

2 rubber bands

6 battery-powered lights

Steps:

1. Prepare the pumpkins for carving by following the directions on pages 16–17. Cut top lids and trapdoors in each one.

2. The large pumpkin will be the main part of your house. Sketch out your design for a door and windows. Transfer the design (*see directions on pages 12–13*) and carve it out by following the carving tips on pages 18–19.

3. One of the small pumpkins will be the house's attic. Draw a sketch for a ghostly window. Transfer and carve it out.

4. The other four small pumpkins will be rooms in the house. Cut four squares into each one to look like windows.

5. Add details such as shutters and windowsills to all of the pumpkins. Do not cut all the way through the shell.

6. To set up your display, find a flat area on the ground. Place the large pumpkin in the middle. Discard its lid. Collect hay or dried grass, and glue it around the top rim of the pumpkin. Place the attic on top. Discard its lid and poke small branches around its top rim like a spooky balcony.

Your haunted house can have doors, windows, shutters, and other details.

Dried grass can make a great thatched roof.

7. Place a room on either side of the large pumpkin. Discard their lids. Place the other two rooms on top of these. Collect hay or dried grass. With a rubber band, fasten the hay to the stem of these pumpkin lids to look like thatched roofs.
8. Poke sticks into the ground in the front of the pumpkin house to look like a fence.
9. Place battery-powered lights in the trapdoors of all of the pumpkins. (Do not use candles for this project, because the hay and sticks are flammable.)

Until Next Year

Your pumpkin creation will last longer outside than inside. But it won't last forever.

Even in the cool outside air, you may notice your pumpkin's face getting wrinkled after a few days. A pumpkin's shell wrinkles and becomes weaker when it loses moisture. Your pumpkin's features and lid may start to sink in. Green and black mold may start growing on the cut areas. Fruit flies may move inside. Mice and squirrels might steal stray seeds.

Since pumpkins are natural, they **decompose** and turn into soil again. Instead of throwing it in the trash can, throw it in a garden or wooded area. Just make sure you take off any unnatural additions, such as clothing, plastic parts, or candy. Don't forget to take the light out from the inside.

You'll have to wait until the next pumpkin season to carve again. In the meantime, why not practice on other fruits? Oranges look a lot like little pumpkins. Or try your carving skills in the summer and create a watermelon jack-o'-lantern!

Glossary

decompose (dee-kum-POHZ) to break down into soil
native (NAY-tiv) having origins in a specific place
nub (NUB) a small bump
pulp (PUHLP) the inner layer of pumpkin that people eat
serrated (suh-RAY-tid) having an edge like a saw
shell (SHEL) the skin and pulp of a pumpkin
skin (SKIN) the outer orange layer of a pumpkin
stems (STEMZ) the parts of pumpkins that attach the fruits to the vine
transfer (TRANS-fur) to move from one place to another

Recipe

TOASTED SEEDS RECIPE

Ingredients
  Pumpkin seeds
  Salt
                    Nonstick cooking spray

Directions
1. Preheat the oven to 325 degrees Fahrenheit.
2. Place the seeds in a bowl and rinse them well with water. Place them on a paper towel and pat dry.
3. Spray a cookie sheet with cooking spray. Place the seeds on the sheet in a single layer. Sprinkle them with salt.
4. Bake for 30 minutes, stirring the seeds on the cookie sheet every 10 minutes with a spoon or a spatula. The seeds are ready when they are golden brown.
5. Let the seeds cool and then eat!

For More Information

Books

Cole, Peter, and Jessica Hurley. *Great Pumpkins: Crafty Carving for Halloween*. San Francisco: Chronicle Books, 2003.

Daning, Tom. *Fun-to-Make Crafts for Halloween*. Honesdale, PA: Boyds Mills Press, 2005.

Esbaum, Jill. *Seed, Sprout, Pumpkin, Pie*. Washington, DC: National Geographic, 2009.

Goldsworthy, Kaite. *Halloween*. New York: Weigl Publishers Inc., 2011.

Web Sites

All About Pumpkins

www.allaboutpumpkins.com

Learn about different kinds of pumpkins.

Pumpkin Carving 101

www.pumpkincarving101.com

Check out some tips for carving interesting pumpkin designs.

University of Illinois Extension—Pumpkins and More

http://urbanext.illinois.edu/pumpkins/default.cfm

Read about the history of pumpkins and find a pumpkin farm near you.

Index

About the Author

Dana Meachen Rau is the author of more than 300 books for children on many topics, including science, history, cooking, and crafts. She creates, experiments, researches, and writes from her home office in Burlington, Connecticut.